Find It!

by Ellen Bari

PEARSON

Scott
Foresman

Editorial Offices: Glenview, Illinois • Parsippany, New Jersey • New York, New York
Sales Offices: Needham, Massachusetts • Duluth, Georgia • Glenview, Illinois
Coppell, Texas • Sacramento, California • Mesa, Arizona

A **globe** is a round model of Earth.

A **map** is a flat drawing of Earth.

A **forest** has many plants and animals.

Look at the map.
The green parts are the forest.

An **ocean** is made of salty water.

Look at the globe.
Globes use blue for oceans.

Glossary

forest an area with many tall trees

globe a round model of Earth

map a drawing of the Earth's surface or part of it

ocean a very large body of salt water